# Look What Rolled In

by Richard C. Lawrence
illustrated by Doug Roy

## Scott Foresman

Editorial Offices: Glenview, Illinois • New York, New York
Sales Offices: Reading, Massachusetts • Duluth, Georgia
Glenview, Illinois • Carrollton, Texas • Menlo Park, California

Long ago, there were no ball games. There were no balls to play with. There was not as much fun!

3

One creature looked up. It saw
something. Then all the creatures
looked. They all saw it.

Look what rolled in! It was new. It was round. Was it fun?

What was it?
The creatures didn't know.
How did it get there?
The creatures didn't know.
What was it for?
The creatures didn't know.

They looked at it.
It sat on the grass.
Was that supposed to be fun?

Then a new creature came.

"Do you like the ball I gave you?" he said. "Let's have fun with this ball!"

"You can throw it!
You can kick it!
You can catch it!"

"We have a big ball.
We have a little ball.
We have a round ball.
We have a not-so-round ball."

"We can play this way!"

"We can play this way!"

"We can play this way!"

13

"Some of us can play.
Or we can all play!
So let's play ball!"

That was long ago. But maybe some of the creatures are still playing. Why not? What was fun long ago is still fun today!